Who Is
Jesus?

Study Guide

Greg Gilbert

with Alex Duke

WHEATON, ILLINOIS

Who Is Jesus? Study Guide

Copyright © 2021 by Gregory D. Gilbert

Published by Crossway
                1300 Crescent Street
                Wheaton, Illinois 60187

Cover design: Dual Identity Design

First printing 2021

Printed in the United States of America

All emphases in Scripture quotations have been added by the authors.

Trade paperback ISBN: 978-1-4335-7394-1

Crossway is a publishing ministry of Good News Publishers.

BP		30	29	28	27	26	25	24	23	22	21
15	14	13	12	11	10	9	8	7	6	5	4	3	2	1

Contents

Study Guide Preface

The entire Gospel of Matthew hinges on a single question. Jesus has just taught his disciples about the false teaching of the Pharisees and Sadducees. "Beware of them," he says. And then Jesus asks his disciples a question: "Who do people say that the Son of Man is?" (Matt. 16:13).

They answer that some say he is John the Baptist or Elijah or Jeremiah or one of the prophets. Jesus then asks the question that changes everything: "But who do *you* say that I am?" (Matt. 16:15). Of course, Peter speaks up. And this time he actually gets it right: "You are the Christ, the Son of the living God" (Matt. 16:16).

It's at this point, Matthew tells us, that Jesus finally begins explaining to his disciples that he's going to die and rise again. It's at this point, in other words, that everything changes. Why? Because there's no question more important than "Who is Jesus?"

Five years ago, Greg Gilbert wrote *Who Is Jesus?* in order to help readers answer this important question. We've written this accompanying study guide to walk you through his book. The structure is not complicated; the goals are not lofty. It simply walks chapter by chapter through the book, forcing you to slow down and consider what you've read.

Who's it for? Any Christian will profit both from Greg Gilbert's book and this study guide. We promise it will stoke your love for Jesus, even if you already know the answer to this important question. But more than that, *Who Is Jesus?* is for those who *don't* know the answer to the question. In other words, this book—and, Lord willing, this study guide—means to be an evangelistic tool. Not exclusively but primarily.

So how should you use the study guide? Alone? Maybe. One-on-one? Perhaps. In small groups? Sure! In short, it doesn't really matter. We hope older church members will use this to disciple new Christians, and Christians will use it to evangelize their friends and family. Beyond that, who knows? Use it however you want. The Lord is honored as his people dwell on his Son.

May God grant many eyes to see, ears to hear, and hearts to be softened to behold the glory of God in the face of Jesus.

Alex Duke
September 2020

1

What Do You Think?

Who Is Jesus? Summary

"Who is Jesus?" is the most important question you can ever consider. And the best place to go in order to consider this question rightly is the pages of Scripture.

Key Texts
John 10:30
John 14:6

1. In your own words, who is Jesus?

2. The Bible is both a historical document *and* the Word of God (pp. 19–20). Do you believe none, one, or both of these claims? Why or why not?

3. We go to the Bible to learn about Jesus. How can we be sure that the Bible is a reliable eyewitness account? (See pages 20–21.)

4. The author says that "Who is Jesus?" is the most important question you'll ever consider (p. 23). Why?

2

An Extraordinary Man, and Then Some

Who Is Jesus? Summary

Some people say Jesus is "just" an ordinary man, or "just" a religious teacher. But does this claim hold up under scrutiny? No, it doesn't. When you focus on Jesus's ministry—both the teaching and the miracles—*and* the response his ministry elicited, it becomes impossible to dismiss Jesus as merely a religious teacher.

Key Texts
Genesis 1:26–28
Matthew 5–7
Matthew 22:15–46
John 11:1–44

1. How did people in Jesus's day respond to his teaching? What might their responses teach us about who Jesus is?

2. Read through Matthew 22:15–46. What did you learn about how the religious leaders of the day treated Jesus? What strikes you about Jesus's teaching?

3. There's a connection between what Jesus teaches in Matthew 22:15–22 and the first chapter of the Bible, particularly Genesis 1:26–28. (See pages 32–33.) What is it? How do these verses from Genesis 1 help you understand that Jesus isn't just talking about taxes in Matthew 22?

4. What do Jesus's miracles have to do with his claims of divinity? (See pages 33–35.)

5. Scripture clearly reports that Jesus taught with authority and performed miracles. But it doesn't stop there. Scripture *also* unpacks why Jesus did these things. Take as two examples the Sermon on the Mount (Jesus's most famous block of teaching) and the resurrection of Lazarus (perhaps Jesus's most famous miracle). What's the *why* behind these two events in Matthew 5–7 and John 11:1–44? (See pages 35–37.)

3

King of Israel,
King of Kings

Who Is Jesus? Summary

The Old Testament is full of kings: David, Solomon, Ahaz, and so on. It's also full of prophecies about a future king who would one day come and rule forever in perfect righteousness. By the time John the Baptizer shows up, the anticipation for this king is palpable, and people begin to wonder: Is he finally coming?

Key Texts
Exodus 4:22–23
2 Samuel 7:14
Matthew 3
Matthew 16:13–20
Luke 19:37–40
Isaiah 9
Isaiah 11
Micah 5

1. Do you think of Jesus as a king? If so, what kind of king do you think he is?

2. What was John the Baptizer's message about Jesus? And what was the proper response? (See page 41.)

3. After Jesus was baptized, the skies opened up and God the Father declared, "This is my beloved Son, with whom I am well pleased" (Matt. 3:17). Why is this significant? What does it have to do with Jesus's kingship? (See pages 42–51.)

4. If Jesus really is a king, then why does he sometimes reject the label? Why does he sometimes acknowledge it? (See pages 43–44.)

5. The author spends a lot of time in this chapter narrating the history of Israel and its kings (pp. 47–51). Why is this vital to understand? What did you learn?

6. The Old Testament is full of surprising language about a coming king. What kind of king do passages like Isaiah 9, Isaiah 11, and Micah 5 pave the way for? (See pages 49–51.)

4

The Great "I AM" . . .

Who Is Jesus? Summary

These days, it's common for well-meaning, intelligent people to say that Jesus isn't God, but he is a wise teacher or a powerful communicator or something benign like that. Do such claims stand up under scrutiny? Looking at the data, do they even make sense?

Key Texts

Exodus 3:14
Psalm 93:4
Matthew 8:23–27
Matthew 14:22–33
Mark 4:35–41
John 8:48–59

1. Read Mark 4:35–41. What surprised the disciples about Jesus's response? What does this tell us about what they thought of Jesus's divinity? (See pages 55–56.)

2. In Matthew 14:22–33, Jesus walks on water. Though that is the most memorable part of this text, what Jesus says is just as crucial to understand the importance of what's going on. What does Jesus say? And why is it so important? (See page 59.)

3. Have you ever heard someone say "Jesus never claimed he was God"? Why is that claim frankly ridiculous? (See pages 60–62.)

4. How do we know Jesus is asserting his identity in John 8:58? What clue gives it away? (See page 62.)

5. When Jesus is calling himself or being referred to as the "Son of God," is he just taking on a title? What else is he referring to? (See pages 63–64.)

6. At the bottom of page 64, the author lists three things Jesus taught about his relationship to his Father. Look up each of the footnoted references (Mark 12:29; Luke 12:10; John 5:18; 8:58; 14:16–17) and then take a moment to reflect on the doctrine of the Trinity. Jot down your reflections in the space below.

7. The author writes, "Once you begin to understand that Jesus is in fact God, and that he is in a unique and exclusive relationship with God the Father, you also begin to understand that if you want to know the God who created you, then you need to know Jesus. There's just no other way" (pp. 65–66). Do you believe this? Do you know God through Jesus or through some other means? What "other means" are most attractive to you?

5

. . . Is One of Us

Who Is Jesus? Summary
It's crucial that we understand that Jesus really was human, because it means that he was not just a visitor to our world. For us humans to be saved, we need Jesus to live not just in our world, but in our flesh.

Key Texts
Luke 4:1–13
Luke 7:1–17
John 11

1. What do Docetists deny? Why does it matter? (See page 67.)

2. At the bottom of page 68, the author writes, "It's crucial that we understand that Jesus really was human, because it means that he was not just a visitor to our world." But why is visiting such a bad thing? Why would a "visit" from Jesus not be what we truly need?

3. What have Christians historically called the act of Jesus becoming fully human? Why is the adverb *fully* so necessary when describing Jesus's humanness? (See page 69.)

4. Stop for a moment and consider not just the historical humanness of Jesus. Consider his *eternal* humanness. (See pages 69–71.) Have you ever dwelt on the fact that Jesus didn't just "become" human, but that he *is* human in this exact moment—now and forevermore? How might this change how you think about Jesus?

5. What kind of man was Jesus? Where in Scripture can you go to answer this question? (See page 72.)

6. Okay, so Jesus became a man. But why? (See pages 73–77.)

6

The Triumph of
the Last Adam

Who Is Jesus? Summary

When Jesus came to earth, he declared war against his oldest enemy: Satan. Their confrontation wasn't just a skirmish, but the culminating battle of a war that had been waged since the beginning of history. In order to see this, we need to return to this beginning of history, and see precisely how the events of Genesis 1–3 connect to the mission and ministry of Jesus.

Key Texts

Genesis 3
Ezekiel 28
Isaiah 14:12–14
Romans 5:18–19

1. Satan seemed to know who Jesus was. So why did he still tempt him?

2. The Bible is clear that Satan isn't an "anti-God" (p. 80). But how does the Bible describe him? What is he like? Where did he come from?

3. How do the answers to the previous question compare to your own thoughts about who Satan is, and what he's like? How might your instincts be shaped more by culture than by Scripture?

4. This chapter spends quite a bit of time narrating the events of Genesis 1–3. Why are these chapters so crucial? What did you learn?

5. How was Satan's temptation in Genesis 3 *not* just a invitation to eat a fruit, but an "attack . . . exquisitely calculated to overthrow everything God had done in the garden" (p. 86)?

6. Describe the cataclysmic effects of the world post-sin. (See pages 90–92.) Is this how you see the world too?

7. What does Adam's sin have to do with you? Does this strike you as unfair?

8. How is Jesus the answer to the problems introduced into the world in Genesis 1–3?

9. Why wasn't Jesus's perfect life enough? Why didn't the story of the Bible stop there?

7

Lamb of God, Sacrifice for Man

Who Is Jesus? Summary

The bare historical fact that a man named Jesus lived and died is relatively uncontroversial. The far more important question is *why* Jesus died. The Bible—from beginning to end, from Genesis to Revelation, from the garden of Eden to the garden of Gethsemane—explains the answer to this question.

Key Texts
Exodus 11:1–7
Exodus 17
Isaiah 53
Matthew 26:17–29, 36–46
John 1:29
Romans 6:23

1. How does the Jewish sacrificial system prepare us to understand Jesus as the Lamb of God? (See pages 97–103.)

2. On page 98, the author writes, "The reason God declared *death* to be the consequence for sin is that it was perfectly fitting and right for him to do so." Do you agree with this statement? Why or why not?

3. How does the death of Christ "beautifully [express] both God's unbending justice *and* his mercy" (p. 99)?

4. The tenth and final plague in Egypt is unique in that it threatened the Israelites too. What might God have been teaching his people through this? (See pages 101–3.)

5. Read through Exodus 17 and Isaiah 53. In what ways do these passages anticipate the work of Jesus?

6. After reading this chapter, how would you answer someone who asked you, "Why did Jesus get baptized?" (See pages 107–9.)

7. Jesus "fell on his face and prayed, saying, 'My Father, if it be possible, let this cup pass from me; nevertheless, not as I will, but as you will'" (Matt. 26:39). What was the Father's answer to his Son's question? (See pages 110–11.)

8. In what ways was Jesus's crucifixion "unusual"? (See pages 113–16.)

8

Resurrected and Reigning Lord

Who Is Jesus? Summary

Jesus's resurrection is the turning point of history. In this chapter, the author narrates the events between Jesus's last breath and the disciples' first realization that Jesus is alive. Everyone needs to reckon with this biblical claim because if it's true, then your response to Jesus cannot be passive indifference.

Key Texts
Mark 16:1–7
John 20
Acts 1:9–11
1 Corinthians 15:14–19

1. What do you think that Saturday was like for the disciples—that day after Jesus's death but before his resurrection?

2. "Did Jesus get up from the dead?" (p. 124) is the most important question in all of history. But why?

3. Why is the ascension of Jesus so significant? (See pages 127–29.)

4. If Jesus really did rise from the dead, if he really is who he claimed to be, then what do you do now?

5. In your own words, what does it mean to "believe" or "have faith" in Jesus?

6. When you believe in Jesus, what good things happen next? (See pages 131–33.)

7. What other action always accompanies true belief? (See page 132.)

A Final Word

Who Do You Say He Is?

Who Is Jesus? Summary
Jesus is alive. Are you ready to respond? You only have a limited amount of time before Jesus's invitation to receive his mercy expires.

Key Text
Hebrews 9:27

1. We end with the question that began this study: In your own words, who is Jesus?

2. If your answer to the above question has changed, why has it changed?

3. If your answer to question 1 is something other than "my Savior and King," then what's holding you back? What questions do you still have? What specific and practical steps can you take to address these questions?

IX 9Marks

Building Healthy Churches

9Marks exists to equip church leaders with a biblical vision and practical resources for displaying God's glory to the nations through healthy churches.

To that end, we want to see churches characterized by these nine marks of health:

1. Expositional Preaching
2. Gospel Doctrine
3. A Biblical Understanding of Conversion and Evangelism
4. Biblical Church Membership
5. Biblical Church Discipline
6. A Biblical Concern for Discipleship and Growth
7. Biblical Church Leadership
8. A Biblical Understanding of the Practice of Prayer
9. A Biblical Understanding and Practice of Missions

Find all our Crossway titles and other resources at 9Marks.org.

More Study Guides from 9Marks

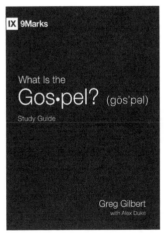

For more information, visit **crossway.org**.

NOTES

NOTES